Engagement

𝔉𝔦𝔯𝔰𝔱 𝔠𝔥𝔲𝔯𝔠𝔥 𝔬𝔣 𝔊𝔬𝔡

Columbia City, Indiana   46725

ENGAGEMENT

David Belgum

EDITOR
Harold Belgum

PUBLISHING HOUSE
ST. LOUIS   LONDON

Concordia Publishing House, St. Louis, Missouri
Concordia Publishing House Ltd., London, E. C. 1
Copyright © 1972 Concordia Publishing House
ISBN 0-570-06761-8

CONTENTS

PART I

WHY ENGAGEMENT?

Maybe you are asking yourself, "If we're going to get married anyway, why mark time in this 'no-man's land'? Let's get on with it."

Do me a favor. Just delay long enough to answer a few questions, and I'll promise not to tell you how we did it in the "olden days." I won't even bore you with how our engagement led to 15 years of fantastically happy wedded bliss (to say nothing of three children).

Don't look now, but in the back of this book there is a Discuss-O-Graph that you and your mate can fill out on a late date when you have nothing better to do. If you have nothing to discuss after that little exercise, you should either get married immediately or not at all; but, of course, that is entirely up to you.

How I would like to get more personally acquainted with you both, but that privilege goes to the pastor who already gave you this little book or to any clergyman who will be glad to talk with you about engagement and marriage. I can think of nothing I enjoyed more in my parish ministry than the premarital counseling, the weddings, and the receptions. Kathie, my wife, was a bridesmaid at one of those gala affairs.

But enough of this getting acquainted; let's get on with the questions. Read these pages alone or with your friend, but in either case be honest—it's a good habit to get into.

CHAPTER 1

What Will You Get Out of It?

Are you surprised I begin with such a selfish question? Let's face it. Instead of the wonderfully *ideal* motive of service, most of us looking forward to marriage have thoughts like the following: "He makes me feel so secure and safe." "I won't be lonesome anymore." "Somehow I'm so happy when I'm with my sweetheart; she's what I've always wanted." Is it wrong to want to get something out of marriage? No.

There is another side to the well-known motto: "It is more blessed to give than to receive." In Holy Communion, or in any sacrament, we are to *receive* a gift of grace. To be grateful for a blessing or a favor from your friend also requires spiritual maturity. Have you known someone so confounded independent you could not do anything for him or her? For genuine give-and-take in marriage a couple has to know what one needs from the other as well as what one can give the other.

As a matter of fact, if you do not feel the need for marriage, don't get married; you'll make an awful spouse. So you must not be embarrassed about admitting that you hope to get something out of the relationship. After all, that is what engagement is for, an opportunity to find out if marriage and family life with this person will be a fulfilling experience. As Jesus said, " . . . that they may have life, and have it abundantly."

"After you, my dear Alphonse" is a game some couples

play. "Oh, no, I don't care what we do tonight; it's whatever you want, Honey," Alex would say in an effort to be 105 percent unselfish. But was it really true that he never had a wish, a preference for this movie over that one; or was he afraid that a conflict might develop and he would lose points with his date. He was married five years before his wife finally told him that she did not appreciate this game. She wanted to feel she was giving him something once in a while too.

Bill took a different approach. His boss at the gas station appreciated his good work and had offered him a chance to become one-fourth partner if he wanted to become that involved. That evening Bill phoned his fiancée, saying, "Sue, I *need* to talk tonight; may I come over?" Like many of us, Bill thinks better out loud, and it was not much fun talking to himself in his own apartment. Now he did not want or need Sue to make up his mind for him, but he did want a chance to discuss pros and cons of the proposition. Also, he simply wanted to share the adventure of this decision. Very likely he will want this same experience again and again in his marriage.

Positive and negative needs. Most people want something wholesome and appropriate out of the marriage relationship, a fairly mature, adult social contract; that is positive. Occasionally one or both partners want something pretty sick, unhealthy, destructive, in other words, negative. Please place a plus or minus sign beside each of the following items—the second person doing the rating should cover the answers of the first party while filling in the blanks:

Man's rating	What I want to get out of marriage	Woman's rating
✗ 1	Security	1 ＋
∕ 2	Ego support	2 ─
✗ 3	Sex	3 ＋

+	4	Criticism	4 +
+	5	Companionship	5 +
−	6	Freedom from responsibility	6 −
+	7	Love	7 +
−	8	Competition	8 −
+	9	Happiness	9 +
−	10	Freedom from parents	10 −
−	11	Someone to take care of me	11 +
+	12	Children	12 +
−	13	Peace and quiet	13 −
+	14	A chance to boss	14 −
+	15	A chance to be supervised	15 +

Some of the above needs or expectations from marriage are mutual, for example, 14 and 15. If one of the pair wants a chance to be boss and the other wants to be bossed, that is a good deal. If both want 14 or both expect to get supervision, there will be fireworks. If both of you see "freedom from responsibility" as positive, I hope you will not be surprised when the loan company comes to repossess your car and furniture. Obviously, the healthier our motivations and the more realistic our expectations and the more wholesome our needs are, the stronger the marriage and the more stable the family life will be.

Engagement is an excellent time to ask oneself seriously and frankly, "What will I get out of it?"

There is much chance for growth in marriage, but some neurotic needs seem to feed on marriage. For example, the classic illustration to which numerous marriage counselors can testify is the pairing of the childlike dependent alcoholic man with a punishing but martyrlike woman. Although she loudly complains of the "cross she must bear," how she must work to support the family, etc., she divorces her husband when he joins Alcoholics Anonymous, sobers up, and works regularly; and then she promptly marries another alcoholic. Why? Because what she really wants from the marriage relationship is the chance to "mother" someone regardless of age.

Those who seek growth and maturity will find ample opportunity for life enrichment. But you need not wait till marriage to start growing. What about now in your court-ship? Do you find that you want positive and compatible experiences? The direction you set now will very likely continue in your marriage.

Engagement is an excellent time to ask oneself seriously and frankly, "What will I get out of marriage?"

Now we turn to the topic with which you thought we would begin our discussion, self-giving love.

CHAPTER 2

What Do You Have to Give?

"He who loses his life [gives it away, shares it] for My sake will find it," said Jesus. Do you believe it? More important, have you tried it? Some spiritual folks believe it is a sin of pride to think that what you have to offer is wonderfully worthwhile.

So maybe you have some weaknesses, some lack of capacity or ability. Look again! You also have some special qualities that made you stand out in a crowd, at least in the eyes of one other person, or you would not be engaged now. Have you thought about these attributes? What do you have to give in marriage and family life? It need not endanger your humility to consider these traits honestly for a moment.

Capacity is important. Maybe your beloved admires your vitality and energy, which you have in abundance and to spare, the capacity to share camping and sports. Or you do not have much physical endurance, but you have a wonderful patience, a steadying influence, the capacity to pour oil on troubled waters, and your partner appreciates it because it's a good counterbalance to an impulsive disposition and a fiery temper. Do you realize what you have to give to the partnership, and does it supplement what the other person needs? If your courtship is developing well, you already have some answers to this question, some hunches as to what the other person appreciates in you.

Experience becomes a part of ourselves which we can

13

share with others. Have you traveled, worked, suffered; or have you gained special experience in handling money, relating to people, or working skills? If so, these can be fine contributions to bring to a marriage partnership. ON ONE CONDITION: Gifts of love and wonderful experiences are to be freely shared and not imposed arbitrarily.

Perhaps you would agree that the left column of approaches would work better in marriage than the right:

Shared Experience	*Imposed Experience*
"I found that a budget helped me stretch my grocery money when we girls had the apartment last year."	"If your father had saved his money like my father, your family wouldn't be in the fix they are today."
"Would you like to walk to class? I find I concentrate better when I've had some exercise."	"You know you wouldn't be so flabby if you'd work out in the gym once in a while. That's how I keep in shape."

GOOD

(Can you think of an example of each type used recently by you or your engagement partner?)

_____	_____
_____	_____
_____	_____

The examples on the left side are suggestions from experience freely shared without demands or criticisms attached. The remarks on the right side have a touch of superiority and judgment that make the listener bristle and counterattack: "I am not"; "Oh, no, you don't"; or "I'll be darned if I'll go along with your stupid suggestion."

In courtship and marriage, gifts of love do not make the receiver feel weak or inferior, but each contribution strengthens the couple, the partnership, the family. St. Paul said it better:

> Love is patient and kind; love is not jealous or boastful; it is not arrogant or rude. Love does not insist on its own way; it is not irritable or resentful; it does not rejoice at wrong, but rejoices in the right. Love bears all things, believes all things, hopes all things, endures all things.   (1 Cor. 13:4-7)

Back to our question: "What do you have to give to a future marriage relationship?" All right, you have thought of something you should give but are not giving because it doesn't come naturally? If you are fairly young, you can change for the better before marriage. Maybe you believe you should give a compliment, moral support in the other person's studies or vocation, a sign of approval in public, etc. But it is difficult; you have not been accustomed to showing gratitude or approval, joy and emotion. Try it! Experiment! See how it works. It may work wonders. Now during engagement is the time to learn new behavior that will support marriage and family life for years to come.

Almost everyone has a lot to give; you are giving much to the courtship relationship now; and you can exercise your generosity and grace even more with some thought and effort. The love of God for us is shown by His continual gifts of grace, a self-giving love. In proportion as we allow this spirit to permeate our lives, we will find giving a natural practice and attitude, especially in courtship and engagement, which lead up to the complete giving of self in married life.

CHAPTER 3

What Have You Got to Lose?

Oh, yes, hopefully you'll gain more than you lose, but you give up some things by getting married. The gal gives up her last name. Letters which used to be addressed to Miss Johanna Heilingdoerfer will henceforth be addressed to Mrs. John Smith; one and the same person maybe, but quite a switch. She may even be a bit touchy about her changed identity.

In college last spring Johanna was known in her own right as women's tennis champion of the Big Ten, but in the fall someone asks who that new gal is, and the reply could well be, "Oh, haven't you met her? She's the wife of the new football coach." The same is true of the wife of the new store manager, the wife of the mayor, etc. It can be quite a shock to a young woman to discover that her identity is measured in the eyes of many in the reflected image of the husband and his vocation. Some women object strongly and counter, "How can this be happening to me toward the end of the twentieth century?"

Men think they are giving up something too. Don't kid yourself. Otherwise, why was that song such a big hit—"Those Wedding Bells Are Breaking Up That Old Gang of Mine"? He gives up the spontaneous, even irresponsible freedom of bachelorhood. Financially he just needed enough gas for his car, some clean laundry, and spending money. Now that he is engaged he wonders about life insurance, job security, and possibilities of buying a house someday. His friends tease him that his "carefree days" are gone forever. Unless he is willing to give up the so-called benefits of bachelorhood, he is not ready to marry.

Does this sound a bit negative? I'd rather have you be a little realistic now during your engagement period than to think naively that you can "eat your cake and have it too." Bachelorhood is simpler in significant ways: scheduling, financing, planning for one instead of two. Go to the movie any time of day or night. Toss your small suitcase in the back of the car and take off for the weekend. Eat or not eat meals as you wish at any time. You're not tied down by being expected to fit into someone else's life and schedule. Yes, life was simple — take it from a bachelor of long standing (married when I was 29) — but I for one was willing to give it up. To paraphrase the self-description of TV's Marshall Dillon, "A chancy life and a little lonely."

Now we come to the other side of "What have you got to lose?" You can lose some gnawing loneliness, the feeling that nobody really misses you, that you don't really belong anywhere like all those other people in families, those settled-down married people. You can lose some anxieties and loose-ends feelings about the future. You can lose the freedom that was not freedom nearly as much as it was irresponsibility. You can lose your childhood and adolescence as you press on to adult responsibilities of marriage and family life. St. Paul had a word for it:

> When I was a child, I spoke like a child, I thought like a child, I reasoned like a child; when I became a man, I gave up childish ways. (1 Cor. 13:11)

Engagement is a good time to make sure one has given up childish ways because "children" shouldn't get married and have children. Adults appropriately get married and have children. There is no suggestion here of giving up fun and laughter, but I think you know what I mean.

Giving up the familiar. We live in a mobile society. Have you considered that if you are still living at home with your parents, getting married means (or should mean) "moving out" like the old pioneers. Maybe you will go to live in a strange part of the city or clear across the mountains. Have you counted the emotional and financial cost of leaving the familiar? Oh, it can be wonderful and adventurous, fun and challenging; but it is an adjustment that you make best with your eyes open. Why do you think mothers and aunts cry sometimes at weddings? Aren't they thinking, "How will our little Susie manage way out there where things are so different and she'll be so all alone" (forgetting for the moment that big, strong George will be there too)?

Compromise is a creative form of "giving up" something. Andy has a thing about skiing in the mountains and for the last five vacations has spent all his free time at that hobby. Janet is crazy about the ocean and has routinely spent her every vacation day and free weekend at the beach. During engagement is the time to experiment with creative compromise. If so, Andy will be willing to give up a weekend of skiing sometime when Janet's friends are having a beach party. Likewise, Janet would be willing at least to see what the mountains look like all covered with snow even if she does not want to become a ski enthusiast. Or they might find a third new activity that strikes their fancy. In any case, the simple fact remains that each will have done less of his or her favorite recreation now that they want to be together. The other solution is for one or the other to give up 100 percent of prized activities and preferences in order to hang onto the other party "at all costs." You might be able to stand that kind of sacrifice for a few dates or even months—but for life? Ugh! Be sure you know the difference between considerate love and slavery. Trying to identify with a beloved person does not require you to lose or cover up your own rightful identity, your true self.

Creative compromise thrives in an atmosphere of both love *and* honesty.

Compromise must not be seen only as two people giving up half of each point, giving in 50 percent each on an argument, or just splitting the difference in anything. Rather a couple growing together in love becomes even more than just the total of both their assets. Maybe that's what they sometimes mean by the phrase, "It's bigger than both of us." It's the kind of arithmetic in which one plus one equals four or even six. So each partner in the couple can discover that recreational life is more than just doubled by combining skiing in the mountains with swimming in the ocean because experiences become richer and broader. New dimensions of experience are discovered through this partnership that would have been missed if Andy had continued to ski in his same rut or Janet had forever splashed at her favorite beach alone.

"What do you have to lose?" Let us end this chapter with the same words with which we began Chapter 2:

"He who loses his life . . . will find it."

CHAPTER 4

A Matter of Timing, or Why Wait?

Engagement is essentially a *period of time*. At this stage in your romance you may look on engagement as *marking time*. If you are very much in love, you often say to yourself, "Why wait? Let's get on with it!" You are impatient with your elders, who insist that certain things take *time*, like getting acquainted. Consider some of the reasons why engagement takes time and why it is important and helpful to wait.

Would you believe that there is a definite relationship between length of engagement and happiness and success in marriage? It's true. Those engaged a year or more are more likely to succeed in marriage. Why do you suppose that is?

Snapshot impressions of another person can tell you something, the impression he or she makes in one moment of time. Thus, in one quick argument you can discover that a particular person has a fiery temper; but you still know nothing of his love of music concealed beneath this rough exterior. One picnic lets you know that your date is a clever cook and also a good sport about a rain-drenched hairdo; but you still know next to nothing about her etiquette and manners at a dinner party. In certain business and professional circles that latter attribute could matter more than the former.

The point is that you cannot see all sides of a person in one or another brief encounter. However, in a year the chances are you will have been together at your beloved's family reunion, as well as at a gathering of your family. Such opportunities will just naturally have included a great variety of associations and settings, successes and failures, competition and cooperation, Christmas and birthday gatherings, as well as helping each other with inventory or waxing the car.

Then there is life-style, something so general and pervasive that couples continue to find out after 20 years of marriage what their partner *really* feels and believes about politics, poverty, honesty, education, vocation, sex, children, religion, ambition, success, criticism, social status, etc. So you see, you can't really wait until you know *all* about your future spouse; but for the purpose of our discussion of why engagement takes some time I hope you are beginning to get the picture. You should get a reel of motion picture film as well as a snapshot. The better you know your future spouse, the more likely you are to enter into marriage with your eyes open, knowing what you're getting into, the more likely you are to be marrying the kind of person you *think* you are marrying.

Impulse buying is no good for seeking a marriage partner. A piped-in music company advertises that merchants who use their soothing sounds in stores encourage "impulse buying." Such a merchant hopes that his customers will not be very careful, discriminating, or sensible about their purchases. But customers who act on whim and buy on the spur of the moment often regret their choice. In romance this is called infatuation. There is some one thing about a person which so catches your fancy that you fall head over heels in love. That may be all right for a few dates at a summer resort on vacation, but for a 40-year marriage it's not enough. In fact you may have found as I have that what seemed to be a real personality attraction in a newfound friend wore thin and even grated on your nerves as time passed. A year's engagement gives you opportunity to look below the surface, time to tell if this human being would wear well over the years in all the varied situations of marriage and family life.

Engagement should give you time enough to be sure you are making the right decision to marry each other. It is also a time for *planning*.

Planning takes time; finding suitable and agreeable housing takes time; getting your bugeting and other thinking changed over from a bachelor ("bachelorette") point of view to a partnership mentality all takes time.

Most couples are amazed at the number of details involved in setting up even a small apartment household.

Much of the equipment and management of their single life had been provided for by their parents, dormitory housekeeper, the landlord of an efficiency apartment, or the army or navy barracks or BOQ (bachelor officers' quarters). But when you return from your honeymoon (more about that later), you'll be on your own—or should be. On your own concerning *everything* from life insurance to light bulbs, from grocery shopping to getting along together.

You wouldn't start a new small company without a lot of planning that takes time—locating a good site, outfitting your shop or warehouse, ordering supplies, checking out the market for your product, getting stationery printed, hiring a secretary or receptionist, getting credit at the local bank, etc.

In Part II, "Have You Talked About It?" there are five areas in which you want to make sure you are ready before getting married. Concerning the length of your engagement you can follow a simple guideline: Have we taken time enough to do all the planning and make all the preparations to get our marriage off to a good, smooth start and establish it on a solid foundation? You be the judge of that.

Among other things, the clergyman who marries you will want to spend some sessions in discussing your forthcoming marriage, or he will suggest a series of group sessions that will be helpful. The couple that hurries into marriage "as soon as possible" misses these resources and takes that many more chances to get off on the wrong foot.

It would be a useless exercise to suggest the matters you ought to tend to and the details and errands that need your attention between now, this very minute, and your wedding day. So why don't you two jot down what plans you yet need to carry out. Include what you like from wedding gown to guest list, from folding money to furniture, from medical examination to marriage license, from etc. to etc.

Things yet to be agreed on:

1. _____.
2. _____.
3. _____.
4. _____.
5. _____.

Things to be done (in order of importance):

1. _____.
2. _____.
3. _____.
4. _____.
5. _____.

Things to be bought:

1. _____ $_____
2. _____ $_____
3. _____ $_____
4. _____ $_____
5. "Skip 5; we can't afford it anyway."

Say, you're going to be busy. Think you'll get it all taken care of in the few months that remain in your engagement?

CHAPTER 5

Why Do Others Care About You Two?

As you two love birds kiss goodnight after a date, you may feel like there are only two people in all the world. You imagine that your romance is an entirely private matter.

Actually you are on stage with quite an audience observing the drama. If Aunt Mathilda were given to betting, she'd wager that the wedding would be before Christmas. Your neighbors comment one way or the other about your romance as do your fellow workers down at the plant or your classmates if you are still in school. More people than you could ever expect are concerned about your courtship, and even society-at-large has a stake in you and your future family.

Why do others care about you two? Because how marriage and family life work out influences the community for better or worse. Wholesome marriages and solid families are an asset to the community; it is as simple as that. On the contrary, sick families, disintegrating families, create a sick society and weakened community.

A survey conducted by a statewide social service agency indicated that most of the problems brought to counselors, pastors, and social workers were *family related:* divorce, child neglect and abuse, alcoholism, delinquency, many personality problems, emotionally disturbed children, and marriage conflicts. The human suffering, the financial loss, and other consequences of disturbed marriages make it quite understandable why society has always been concerned about the success of marriage and family life. Hence the marriage and divorce laws, the legal supports for family solidarity, the safeguards against infidelity and alienation of affection, the guarantees of privacy, the moral expectation that parents will be financially and spiritually responsible for their children, and that husband and wife can be counted on as a stable team "till death us do part."

You can take one of two views toward society's concern for your blossoming romance and your future marriage. You can look upon it as a lot of paternalistic nonsense and interference with your freedom, or you can say to yourself, "I'm sure glad other people are as eager as I am that my marriage will succeed." The social facts won't change one way or the other, but the attitude you both take will make a whale of a lot of difference in your outlook and your relationship with both sets of parents, relatives, and friends. It will also influence how you handle the "bureaucratic red tape" of marriage license people at city hall, requirements of a medical examination, policies of the local parish concerning the wedding, and a dozen other things that could "bug" you. Remember that if you are eager for a successful marriage and a good home, society is on your side.

The church shows her concern and willingness to help by offering premarital counseling to couples approaching marriage. Seek out this opportunity early rather than late in your engagement. This is more than checking the pastor's schedule and making sure the church is not otherwise occupied at the time you wish to set for your wedding. The clergyman may want to visit with you three times or so to talk about the topics following this section (Chapters 6 – 10) as well as anything else you may have on your minds.

The advantage of having these sessions several weeks or even a couple months ahead of the marriage is that you can deal with any problems or unresolved issues that might be brought to light as you get into these topics.

A good suggestion here is that you expose yourself to the opinions and reactions of others. One study revealed that an excellent indicator of success in marriage was what one's relatives and friends thought about the match during courtship. You have one image of yourself; your family and many acquaintances each have their own unique image of you, your fiancé(e), and how you seem to fit together. If you will expose yourself to their impressions and encourage their sharing their feelings with you, you get many perspectives about yourselves as a couple, rather like looking at your new outfit in a clothing store's combination mirrors where you can see yourself in profile and from the back.

"Hold it!" you say. "What if I should discover we are not 'meant for each other'? That would mean the end of our engagement. The wedding, now only seven weeks away, would be off and I'd just die of embarrassment."

"Well," a calm uninvolved bystander might say, "wouldn't you rather know now than later that you are not 'meant for each other,' as you say?"

"No, a thousand times no!" you reply in tears. "If I don't get married now, I'll be a bachelor (or spinster as the case may be) for the rest of my miserable life."

Well, then your choice seems very simple: whether to be miserable single or miserable married.

You strike me on the other cheek also. As you rush from the room, I hear you saying over your shoulder, "Leave me alone, you brute! If he's still in, I'm going to talk to my premarital counselor about those five topics that brought up this argument in the first place."

So why not just turn to the next section of this helpful little book, Part II, "Have You Talked About It?"

HAVE YOU TALKED ABOUT IT?

There are hundreds of things you have both talked over already and countless concerns you could explore further. Each couple has its unique mutual dialog. My own experience with couples contemplating marriage and a survey of writings on the subject indicate that the following five areas of discussion are shared almost universally: _social, economic, personality_ (psychological), _physical_ (including sex), and _religious_. These are not listed in any order of importance nor will you necessarily take them up in this sequence. Begin wherever _you want_ to begin or _need_ to begin.

The purpose of dealing with these subjects or dimensions of marriage is to iron out any difficulties or, put positively, to make sure that each of these areas will be as rewarding and fully a part of your life together as possible. Please do not think the purpose is negative just because they are stated as possible problems, but getting "problems" out in the open is more realistic than a Polyanna approach. If you are in love, chances are that there is already enough positive thinking what with the candlelight and roses and all. It is my job to see that you have faced hurdles as well as opportunities. The following outline puts it in a nutshell.

Areas of Discussion	*Problems Disrupting* *Family Life*

(Working through these topics . . . may prevent . . . these problems from getting out of hand)

1. *Social* Relations
   Family
   Friends
   Background

   Interpersonal Conflict
   In-law tensions
   Isolation
   Clash of loyalties

2. *Economic* Questions
   Vocation
   Finances
   Values

   Financial Distress
   Vocational acceptance
   Budgeting problems
   Standard of living

3. *Personality Factors*
   Maturity
   Openness
   Health

   Emotional Instability
   Neurotic outbursts
   Suspicion
   Incompatibility

4. *Physical* Aspects
   Sex information
   Masculinity-femininity
   Planned parenthood

   Sexual Problems
   Fear and anxiety
   Role conflict
   Rejection of children

5. *Religious* Perspective
   Faith and beliefs
   Morality and ethics
   Practices and
      membership

   Meaninglessness
   Conflict over convictions
   Standards of behavior
   Mixed-marriage conflict

CHAPTER 6

Social Relations

What has been the reaction of others to your engagement? Has it been mostly "Congratulations!" or "You're kidding?" What about your folks, your elders, your peers?

Next question: Has it changed your social relationships? Have you forsaken parties where you used to go eagerly to meet new acquaintances and retreated into a little world of your own? If so, is that what you expect to continue doing when you are married? What is the ideal social pattern for a couple? Is it membership in groups, or being together in their own home most of the time? Are you glad your loved one has friends and is popular, or does it make you very jealous and insecure?

Cultural background is far more important than we would like to believe in our age of democracy and supposed equality. Let me illustrate it by the following case:

Nels and Jenney met at a small denominational college sponsored by an ethnic group in the Midwest. He was from Maine and she from Milwaukee. They seemed to hit it off from Freshman Week right on. In their junior year she invited him to spend Christmas at her lovely home overlooking Lake Michigan. Her father was an affluent insurance executive who showed every hospitality to Nels, who in turn appreciated the royal treatment and reciprocated with fairly good etiquette. Nels and Jenney went to the same church, enjoyed many of the same recreational and social functions. It came as a great shock to Jenney when they were married after their graduation from college that Nels was content to settle down in Maine on the meager potato farm with its run-down house while he did a little accounting on the side in town. Jenney was amazed to see how Nels' mother kept house, what she would settle for as the "good life."

Before we are too surprised that this couple had not considered their social and cultural backgrounds, let us analyze the conditions under which they courted. All the men students lived in the same dormitory rooms, had their shirts laundered at the same commercial laundry in town, ate in the same co-ed dining hall. On dates they went to the same picnics, pizza parlors, root beer stands, and Student Union dances. Their similarities were more conspicuous than their differences.

Ever since knowing Nels and Jenney, I have asked couples whether they have been in each other's parental homes. Have they met at least some of the brothers or sisters? The one or two hundred dollars spent on such a trip, even from Milwaukee to Maine, could be well worth it. Don't get me wrong; I do not for a moment say that a person should not marry someone from a distinctly different socioeconomic or cultural background. It is, however, important to know all these things beforehand. Then one knows what adjustments will be needed.

> For which of you, desiring to build a tower, does not
> first sit down and count the cost, whether he has
> enough to complete it?   (Luke 14:28)

It is up to you once you know the price of the adjustments you will have to make in your social and cultural setting after marriage. Go in with your eyes open and you will both be better off and happier for it.

If you are a broad-minded person open to new experiences, you can find differences quite charming: new ways of preparing food, different ways of celebrating Christmas, folk songs and customs you otherwise would have missed, a chance to appreciate another temperament and life-style. Courtship and engagement is the time to find out if you want to include these strange and new patterns into your own life-style. But please don't marry hoping that your spouse will leave all this behind. So, you see, the old quip is still quite true that you do marry the other person's family in a sense, because the family has gotten under that person's skin. If your beloved is an orphan, you should expect to find some of the orphanage or foster-home experiences in the luggage too.

Engagement is a time for getting to know the other person in depth. That includes the past, the successes and failures, the associations with the high school band or football team, the joiner or the isolate as the case may be. This calls for honesty about social relationships and what they mean. If there is a part of your social background that embarrasses you, by all means *out with it!* Do not hope that for 40 years of married life your spouse will never find out that your father was unemployed for a while, or that your mother spent a year in a mental hospital, or that your uncle is an alcoholic or a millionaire or whatever.

One clergyman whom I counseled had been a great athlete in a university. Unusually dark and handsome, he married the blondest gal he could find. He suffered all kinds of emotional problems and even a psychosomatic skin condition because he had hidden from his wife the fact that he was one fourth American Indian. There was something missing in their engagement relationship. To make a long story short, she loved him even more once he started being honest. But if that ethnic-cultural-racial factor would have broken up their engagement, they should not have gotten married anyway.

What are some of the specific items that might come

under this category of social relations? You may add to this list, but meanwhile check off the items you are sure about (plus or minus).

_____ 1. Social class (slum or country club set)
_____ 2. Father's employment (profession, day labor, etc.)
_____ 3. Education of family members (and how they feel about it)
_____ 4. Type of home and furnishings (taste and atmosphere)
_____ 5. Cultural interest (concerts, books, TV programs)
_____ 6. Racial (black, white, yellow, red, etc.)
_____ 7. Religious-ethnic (German-Lutheran, Irish-Catholic, etc.)
_____ 8. Neighborhood of residence (Would you like to live there?)
_____ 9. Recreational interests and hobbies (or "work addict")
_____ 10. Social attitude (bigoted or tolerant)
_____ 11. Attitude toward authority (in the home and out of it)
_____ 12. Matriarchal or patriarchal (Who wears the pants in the family?)
_____ 13. Political leanings (conservative or liberal)
_____ 14. Social consciousness (working for civil rights and migrant workers, etc., or content with status quo)
_____ 15. Attitudes toward entertaining in the home (if not, why?)

You see there is no end to this list.

Now remember, you must check the list twice; once for yourself and your family and once for your partner, who should likewise check it twice. How else can you get a healthy respect for each other's differences?

The plot thickens. Cindy was so sure that any boyfriend would look down on her when he found out that her father was a janitor in a university building and carried his lunch box to work that she always represented her father as being "an engineer with the university; he heats and cools the buildings." So she started playing a little game of "I think I know what you're thinking; and that's bad news, because if I were you, I wouldn't like me in the first place, my father being a janitor and everything." It is very difficult to keep score in this kind of game.

It is much better during engagement to play a game called "This is who I am; this is where I came from; and this is where I am going. Now if there are any questions, I'll be glad to answer them." For this kind of game you do not even need an umpire. And the score does not really count because everyone wins. And husband and wife who began this game in their courtship can play it all their life, even with their children.

By the way, what kind of dates are you having now during your courtship—double dates, parties, plays and concerts, sports, or solitary necking sessions? Do you have friends in common, and do you like each other's friends? What about the attitude of your future in-laws toward your romance and prospective marriage—"Can hardly wait" or "Can hardly wait for you to get lost"? Have you both talked and shared your real feelings about the family as a social unit, the function of the family, and of mother and father roles? These all involve social relations attitudes right now and have great significance for your future marriage and family life.

Chapter 7

Economic-Vocational Values and Goals

Here we are concerned about more than how much money the man of the house will earn on the job. A more basic question is: Does he have a *vocation?* What does he think is so important, socially significant, challenging, or just plain fun that he wants to spend eight hours a day doing it until he is 65? Maybe you think this is idealistic and unimportant just as long as a fellow is "working steady." One couple I saw did not think it mattered that the man hated his present job and had lost three jobs in the last year. He had worked every day as he switched jobs. Since one study indicated that a third of the divorces involved nonsupport, it might have been wise for the woman involved in this particular couple to wait and see if her man could hold a job.

Vocation is a spiritual as well as an economic matter. The Christian ideal is that a person feels called to some task or service to his neighbor in gratitude for the blessings he has received in his life. Such a person has a sense of stewardship over the talents, capacities, and opportunities that are his. This does not mean that he is so naive that he forgets about his salary, "for the laborer deserves his wages," according to Jesus (Luke 10:7). But it does mean that a man's vocation is always more than his "job."

Finding one's niche is not as easy as it sounds. St. Paul told the Philippians (4:11): "I have learned, in whatever state I am, to be content." But our society is based on an economy of discontent. Trade in your fan for an air con-

34

ditioner and your small car for a larger one. Take more training so you can "better yourself." Out of this approach has come the "Peter principle": A person is promoted to the level of his *in*competence. This means that we keep on trying to be promoted till we finally hit a level of job that is too difficult for us and then we level off, staying on as long as possible at this job for which we are unsuited. In our culture a paint salesman is somehow supposed to keep on coveting the position of sales manager and beyond him that of the manager of the district office. It may be an ambitious wife who is the driving force behind this "success."

The other side of the coin is the moral responsibility each person should feel to use to the full the energy and capacities with which he is endowed. So a person who has the potential to be a great surgeon should not be content as an assistant to the orderly on the ward. He owes it to sick people to become a doctor.

Why this little sermon on work, especially since it may not apply to you at all? Once an investigation was made into the question of job satisfaction. What do you suppose mattered most to the workers? Not money, not working conditions, but what the wife thought of the man's job. Was she proud of him? Was she content that he was doing something worthy of his capacities and honorable in the eyes of the community? A man needs this as much as a wife needs to hear her husband's approval of her homemaking and motherhood.

Will the wife say of her husband, "My man is a fine carpenter; when he puts in a stair rail it stays put." Or, "I'm proud of my husband's law practice, but even more pleased that he donates some time each week to the Legal Aid Society."

Working wife. "Ah," you say, "what about the liberation of women and their equality in the labor force?" It is very common for the young wife to continue teaching, nursing, clerking in a store, or at her secretary's desk after she gets married. My wife worked till our first child was born. We lived on my salary as a teacher and saved her salary toward the down payment on our first house. Of utmost importance in vocation and money matters is the team approach, the mutual agreement to whatever arrangement is made.

You cannot possibly plan out all the work alternatives for a wife any more than you can for a husband between marriage and retirement. Things change. When the youngest child gets along in school, say toward junior high, the house may begin to feel a bit empty all day for the housewife. The wife who never thought she would want to work again now gets restless and bored. Who can anticipate the ideal life-style 10, 20, 30 years from now? But at least we can talk about possible alternatives and how each of us feels about them. Mutual discussion and frank sharing of opinions contribute to compatability in marriage and good teamwork. Practice this in your engagement, and do not just say what you think the other person wants to hear. Discuss all the angles, implications, and consequences; the pros and cons of the "working wife" and "working mother."

Budgeting may be your strong or your weak point. Who should write out the checks? What is legitimate fun and what is wasteful foolishness? Do I need to supplement the "fringe benefits" which my employer provides with further life insurance, major medical coverage (and does my policy cover pregnancy?), savings plan for the children's education as well as our retirement income, etc.? Do you need a last will and testament before any children arrive on the scene? What is an appropriate amount to set aside for clothing, food, entertainment, vacation, church and charity, Christmas and birthday presents for relatives (and which relatives? oh, oh).

Some people are systematic by nature, others spontaneous and free-wheeling. If you and your fiancé(e) approach money quite differently, first make sure you are talking about the same thing. Sometimes money stands for something else like self-regard, authority (back to who signs the checks), masculinity, success, etc. It is a lot like automobiles. Some use them for transportation, others for social status, many for both. Not that we can always be 100 percent sure of our motives, but we can at least try to be talking about the same thing.

Sometimes when we are planning a budget, we are really talking about values in life, priorities, moral responsibility. To what do I want to commit myself and how much? That is really what a loan or installment buying amounts to.

Perhaps you have discussed how much money you should have in your checking account. (Oh, yes, a joint checking account or "his" and "hers" checkbooks?) Couples range from one extreme to the other. I have heard of a couple that thought they should wait to get married until they had saved enough money to buy a house for cash. Others do not know where the first month's rent will come from. Hopefully you fall somewhere between these two extremes. Mostly, it depends on how much anxiety you can tolerate or how much security you need. It is not really the best way to simply guess at what is appropriate in your own unique situation; but, again, try to come to an agreement between yourselves. It may be one of your first opportunities to experiment with compromise, a useful technique in marriage.

Standard of living—now there's a phrase that is tossed about a good deal these days. We continually worry about the possibility that some other country might have a higher standard of living than the "American way of life." On a smaller scale, we wonder if we should keep up with the Joneses. How independent are you at setting yourself a standard of living? Give it some thought. How is it that one family frets and stews about money when they have a $30,000 annual income, and the next family lives quite at ease and content on less than half? The first family is mortgaged to the hilt, and then some, on a luxury house; their speed boat is bought on time (at 1½% per month, that's 18% interest); they have the most expensive model auto they can find, also on as large a bank note as they could negotiate. Frankly, they feel like they are in poverty with their backs against the wall.

Chances are that you have either accepted the values and standards of your family (and your future spouse the same), or you may have reacted violently. "My folks scrimped and saved till it was sickening. When we are married and on our own, we are going to 'live it up.'" Or just the opposite: "The creditors and other wolves were always at our door. One thing's for sure; I want money in the bank."

You can assume responsibility for your own lives, you two lovers. As the saying goes, "Be your own man; do your own thing." You are starting a new chapter, a new family, a new home; let it be your own. Create your own standard of living according to the best insights you can muster. Hammer out your own way of life, your own priorities, your own reasons for buying or not buying something. Be open to advice and the experience of others, but when the chips are down, *you two* decide whether you are going to rent or own your home, go here or there for vacation.

Just remember that the simple rules of arithmetic apply to the sincere and the foolish, the wise and the simple. There are still 10 dimes in a dollar. No matter how sophisticated you are, 1½% monthly interest payments still mean that you paid $118 for that thing marked $100 in the store.

CHAPTER 8

Personality: Who Are You?

If someone gave you a blank sheet of paper and asked you to fill it up with the answer to one simple question: "Who are you?" what would you say about yourself? If you hesitated or were too brief, the examiner would press you with, "Yes, but go on; what else makes up YOU? What are you *really* like?" How you replied would be revealing.

A job-conscious person begins his answer by saying, "I am a nurse" or "I am a carpenter; that's who I am." Another person is first conscious of something else; being French-Canadian, being 21 years old (meaning I'm old enough to vote, to marry, to drink on my own), being black (black is beautiful), being a graduate of so-and-so college, being an apprentice linesman with the telephone company, being beautiful or ugly, being too short or too tall, being a child of God, etc.

Now, suppose we ask your date after a party to do the same, describe who you are and what you are like. You might think you are fairly timid, whereas your partner feels you are too forward. One considers himself to be optimistic and happy-go-lucky, while the other sees him as rather cautious and even suspicious.

Actually, you have several "personalities," a bit like seeing yourself from several angles or different points of view as follows:

1. Husband	1. Wife
(as he wants to be seen) ideal image	(as she wishes to be thought of) ideal image

2. Husband   2. Wife
   (as he thinks of himself)   (as she perceives of
   self-concept   herself) self-concept

3. Husband   3. Wife
   (as others really see   (as seen by others)
   him) social role   social role

4. Husband   4. Wife
   (as he really is)   (as she really is)
   objective fact   objective fact

Obviously the ideal marriage is between husband #4 and wife #4. Couple #1 lives in a dream world; #2 lives in a limited world uncorrected by outside evidence; #3 relies entirely on public relations, as Reisman termed them, "other directed." On second thought, maybe all four views have their place as long as we keep them in balance.

Marriage is not the joining of two disembodied spirits; it is the "correlation" of two personalities. Personality consists of temperament, physique, vital energy, intelligence, beliefs, emotions, physical and mental health, and ways of behaving.

Consider the approach of two persons to problems. When Susan is confronted by a problem, she begins by having a good cry; second, she ponders why all this tragedy should be happening to her of all people; third, she appeals to someone else for help. John is more direct. First, he analyzes the situation and divides the problem into its three natural parts; second, he tries several alternate plans if the first approach does not work; third, he consults someone else only after he has used up his own resources within a reasonable period of time. If John and Susan have an engagement in any true sense of the word, they will soon discover how differently they approach problems. But then, they were not identical twins in the first place.

Maturity comes to each of us at different stages of our personality development. Janice had always been old for her years. As the oldest child in a poor family where her mother worked, it fell to her lot to be more than baby-sitter, practically a mother substitute. Now she was 24 and engaged to the foreman of a cement crew, a big, husky fellow two years her senior. Unfortunately for Janice, she still had this basic approach of feeling that she should mother everyone in sight; but her fiancé wanted a wife and not another mother. Two courses of action were open to Janice when their engagement was breaking up: get some counseling to find out how she could change her relationship and act as one adult to another adult instead of acting as a parent to a child, or she could find another man who wanted, needed, and appreciated a rather maternal figure to take care of him. There are many marriages like that that work out beautifully. Sometimes it seems a bit humorous to others when Miss Amazon marries Casper Milquetoast; but they can be quite compatible. It certainly was not going to work out for Janice and her construction crew foreman.

Maturity is an elusive goal. It takes a good deal of maturity not to *get* married but to *stay* married. Marriage itself is a maturing experience, to say nothing of parenthood. What I am suggesting you two ask yourselves is this: Are you two the kind of combination that will help each other to continue maturing so that each of you may become a more wholesome, loving, fully developed personality — what the church means by "growing in grace." This means you are willing to learn from each other, to challenge each other, to help each other because of a deep and abiding love for each other. If your engagement is succeeding, you have already found this to be the case; and it looks increasingly like marriage will be for you a continuation of this wonderful maturing relationship.

There is a bitter-sweet story of a woman who was intimidated, frustrated, inhibited, and depreciated by her husband the whole 40 years of their marriage. Oh, they stayed married all right, but you should have seen her mature and blossom when he died at age 65. She developed into really quite an interesting person in her old age. Wonder how different both of them might have been if they'd had a different relationship in their engagement, or maybe they did not feel engagement was necessary. What a pity that this woman marked time for 40 years of married life when it should have meant a period of rich personality development.

Honesty and self-disclosure bring people who were meant to be together into a closer relationship of fellowship and communion. Honesty and self-revelation separate people who were not meant to be together. Since the purpose of engagement is to discover whether or not you two should spend your whole life together in marriage, it is important to make use of this period of testing.

Many engagements and courtships skip this important testing because of fear of breaking up. Hence, if he/she knew how I *really* felt about sex, children, religion, politics, my parents, minority groups, war, clothing styles, money, manners, alcohol, football, etc., we would never get married. But you see what this implies: the safest thing will be to keep all these possible sources of conflict under cover during our entire married life. It will also mean that I will have to lie a little bit all the time to keep peace in the family; and I suppose my spouse should be expected to lie most of the time too then. Ouch! What a grim life! Reflect a bit on what Jesus thought of hypocrisy as a way of life.

When a relationship is developing in a wholesome and healthy way, we find that we are getting to know each other more and more fully and intimately all the time. For one thing we discover it is safe to do so because the other person lets us know such self-disclosures are welcome and helpful. It is as simple as that. If I know my girl friend detests bull fights and I really love her, I will not plan our honeymoon as a tour of Mexico with tickets purchased in advance to see a different matador fight a bull each day. But if she never tells me how she feels or what she thinks about anything, how would I know?

To put the shoe on the other foot (always a good exercise in engagement and marriage), take the case of Jack and Edith. Jack was very proud of his fiancée and had first been attracted by her gorgeous figure. He was pleased to find that her personality and social graces matched her female form. But in his mind one dark cloud hung over their relationship. He thought she was awfully free with her charms. At parties he was sure she danced too close to other fellows, but felt he could not speak of it for fear of being branded "jealous" or a "prude." Nevertheless, it bothered him that she took such delight in men's stares when she wore a stunning gown with a very low-cut neckline. He just swallowed his resentment. The result was a series of spats, but never about this issue. Usually the argument would be about something else on the surface, an indirect way Jack used for handling his anger and fear of losing her. Finally he blurted out his accusations and a scrappy fight separated them for a time. In the long run it cleared the air. Once they both understood how the other felt and what certain behavior meant to each of them, they made a very good adjustment. But the most important lesson they learned was a new *method* of handling differences, conflicts, and problems. Their new relationship was better than ever, and their marriage stronger for it.

Forgiveness is so essential a part of the Christian way of life that we would do well to ask if it is also applicable in engagement and marriage. It is the other side of the coin and the counterpart of self-disclosure, which sometimes is basically a confession. <u>Confession without forgiveness</u> (when moral offense or sins are involved) <u>is cruel and incomplete.</u> When the grace of God is at work in two lives, forgiveness follows repentance and confession to round out and complete the circle of reconciliation. Since we are all human, we need to live in an atmosphere of forgiveness and acceptance. To expect never to need forgiveness or never to be willing to forgive is hardhearted and arrogant.

Progressive self-disclosure develops over a lifetime. The following balance sheet gives some impression of how we get to know each other by stages:

Percentage of Personality Revealed

(approximately of course)

	Known	Unknown
First date		
Steady dating		
Early engagement		
Late in engagement		
Honeymoon		
Married five years		
Married 25 years		

Many other preferences and attitudes and behavior patterns make up your personality. You need to blend your two personalities into a new pattern so that *two may become one.* You need some agreed-upon schedule of work, rest, play, lovemaking, and worship. Is one of you an early-to-bed type and the other a night owl? The one likes to plan by Wednesday what to do on the weekend, while the other likes to "take it as it comes — see what turns up"?

Finally, if this is not getting ahead into the next chapter, what do you think is appropriate to woman and what is the man's role? Customs and social expectations change, but I am not so concerned with generalizations as I am about you two and how you will fit together. Is it essential for a "gentleman" to open the car door, or is that an outmoded chivalry? Is it beneath a man's dignity to dry dishes or accompany a woman on a shopping trip? How about feeding and bathing the baby? Raise other questions between you. Granted there is a tendency today toward more interchangeable roles and less clear-cut distinctions between the sexes, the important point is that you two work out relationships and mutual expectations that you can live with enjoyably and effectively.

CHAPTER 9

Sexuality in Marriage

Following up our discussion of getting to know a person in an increasingly meaningful sense, we are reminded that in the Old Testament the Hebrew term for sexual intercourse was "to know." We read in Genesis that "Adam *knew* Eve his wife, and she conceived and bore Cain" (4:1). It is true that in sexual intercourse husband and wife communicate realities about each other and their relationship in a nonverbal way that cannot be put into words. Communicating trust, giving of joy and pleasure, an overwhelming sense of being wanted and needed, these emotional exchanges go far deeper than any discussion of ideas. This is what makes the husband-wife relationship unique.

> Therefore a man leaves his father and his mother
> and cleaves to his wife, and they become one flesh.
> (Gen. 2:24)

Sex education is becoming so common in churches and schools that chances are you are already well informed about the nature of male and female sexuality. In case you want to read some straightforward and clear explanations of what you should know about sex before you get married, let me pause right here to cite three of the many available:

Sex Without Fear, S. A. Lewin and John Gilmore. Medical Research Press, 136 West 52d St., New York, N. Y. 10019

A Doctor Speaks on Sexual Expression in Marriage, Donald M. Hastings (a psychiatrist). Little, Brown and Co., Boston.

A Doctor's Marital (Sex) Guide for Patients (regular or rhythm edition), Bernard S. Greenblat. Budlong Press Co., 5428 North Virginia Ave., Chicago, Ill. 60625. (Part of a series available only through professional sources; other titles such as *A Doctor Talks to 5-to-8-Year-Olds, A Doctor Talks to 9-to-12-Year-Olds,* and *What Teenagers Want to Know,* all excellent.)

Knowledge *about* sex is useful and can prevent some strange misconceptions (if you will pardon the pun) — girls thinking they might get pregnant from kissing or the druggist's son telling his girl friend to take a pill just before they had intercourse. But factual knowledge is no guarantee of the good life either. The most incompatable couple I have ever known were a doctor and nurse who had all the facts. Furthermore, some of the currently popular attitudes toward sexual morality, in my opinion, will be shown in the long run to be a violation of basic personality and family needs.

More important is the way all this information fits into your own understanding of yourself, your acceptance of your own sexuality. Have you accepted your own sexuality, and do you believe it is basically a good thing to be what you are? Or do you wish you were of the opposite sex? Do you envy the opposite sex, "which has so many advantages or privileges"? If so, you will find it difficult to fulfill your own sex role and a burden to fulfill the sexual needs of your spouse.

Hopefully you have a positive attitude toward your body as a holy part of creation.

> Do you not know that your body is a temple of the
> Holy Spirit within you, which you have from God?
> You are not your own; you were bought with a price.
> So glorify God in your body.   (1 Cor. 6:19-20)

If you have any hang-ups, anxieties, unresolved questions about sexual intercourse, childbirth, planned parenthood, etc., please talk them over *very frankly* with some counselor *before* you get married. Seek out a physician, guidance counselor at your school, pastor, public health nurse, but do find someone whom you trust and with whom you can share your concerns and misgivings, since these people have had much experience resolving just such questions and will not think any less of you for coming with what you might consider "stupid" or embarrassing problems. You might want to read one of the books mentioned on page 47 before your conference or between interviews.

Natural instinct draws man and woman together even without charts and diagrams, without the knowledge of physiology and biochemistry. Mostly, we have to spend much time discussing sex to *re*educate people, to correct mistaken notions, to overcome learned fears and false modesty. The simple act of coitus is performed very effectively by dogs, monkeys, and cattle with hardly any schooling at all. It is precisely because man is more than animal, or, if you will, a social and moral animal, that sexuality becomes so complex that we need to discuss it and understand all the consequences of this powerful instinct.

Social-emotional aspects of sex, ah, that is what makes sex for man an entirely different ball game from what it is for animals. Animals do not have to contend with illegitimate births, criminal abortions, venereal disease, infidelity (except in some species), guilt feelings, etc. But, then, animals also do not have the rich association of family life, the many-faceted shared love relationship with a spouse, the emotional involvement, the long period of parent-child nurture with its fascinating buildup and satisfactions.

Sex can be either a symptom or a cause. Wonderful consideration and thoughtfulness can build up an attitude of tenderness to the point where husband and wife wish to consummate their love at the highest level of shared experience, intercourse. Or, on the other hand, a wonderful experience of sex can encourage more appreciation of each other and further show of understanding and willingness to do other things for each other as well.

One marriage counselor said that when he found a man who had gotten an extramarital affair going with his secretary, he usually assumed that he was having business or professional reverses. In other words, he was using sex to prove that he was still competent at something. On the contrary, a prolonged bad sexual relationship with its tensions and frustrations not only sends the husband off to work with a less than ideal self-image and state of mind and makes the mother a nervous nag toward the children, but it can actually be harmful for physical and mental health.

Getting ready for married sex is part of the purpose of engagement. It is assumed that there will be a greater show of affection in the later stages of engagement, surely, than during casual and random dating. Those who hop into bed on the first date may never discover nor be interested in learning that there can be more to sex than orgasm. If you have been oh-so-casual about your sexual relationships, I suggest that you have some thorough discussions with a counselor. You will be needing it as preparation for marriage just as much as the person mentioned above who was so naive as to think kissing caused pregnancy. Some of the most sexually maladjusted young people I have known are very sophisticated college students; and what is more, they have not used their engagement to grow or gain perspective in this area.

Then, how to get ready? Again the clue is communication. Consider the problem of increasing intimacy, necking or petting as courtship builds up in intensity toward marriage. It is like trying to hold back a team of horses that last mile who want to get to the barn before the storm comes. It is pleasurable. Now let's hold this romantic mood and move it into a discussion.

Just because dealing with our sexual instinct is not easy is one reason why engagement should not be prolonged unnecessarily. Our society does not help much by requiring increasingly long preparation for certain careers leading to financial independence.

Change of pace, change of setting, change of dating patterns can help to take some of the intensity off the sexual aspect of courtship. The couple that plans to sit necking in a parked car two hours every night is putting undue stress on themselves and in a sense asking for trouble.

At the risk of reactivating the generation gap, I can only add the experience of many marriage counselors and writers in the field of courtship and engagement who agree that premarital intercourse brings more problems than it solves. This in spite of statistics that indicate it is on the increase. But, then, notice that divorce rates and violence and many other questionable factors are also statistically on the increase in our society. Rather than get preachy about this matter, just let me conclude with some items which you may check true or false:

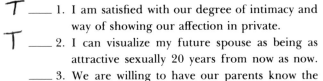

T ____ 1. I am satisfied with our degree of intimacy and way of showing our affection in private.

T ____ 2. I can visualize my future spouse as being as attractive sexually 20 years from now as now.

____ 3. We are willing to have our parents know the

degree of our intimacy.

F ___ 4. We have talked about how many children we want to have and how to arrive at that number through planned parenthood.

F ___ 5. We have discussed how often we might wish to have intercourse on the average.

F ___ 6. Sex is necessary, but the thought of it is slightly distasteful and messy.

T ___ 7. I have handled any guilt involved over sexual behavior that I did not really approve of but participated in anyway.

F ___ 8. The main reason for setting the wedding date when we have is that we just cannot stand the sexual frustration of not being married.

F ___ 9. Childbirth is a frightening experience.

CHAPTER 10

Religious Perspective

Maybe you have not noticed, but religious perspectives have popped up in many places during our discussion: in connection with social relationships, vocation and values, what it means to be a person and in communion with another person, etc. By this time in your engagement you surely know many of the major convictions, beliefs, moral values, and philosophy of life that your loved one holds. You may share many or all of them.   Do I ?

Superficial couples (and this has nothing to do with education or intelligence) are willing to ask and answer only the smallest and simplest questions: "Should we go bowling or to the movie?" "Do you like my blue dress or the pink one with ruffles better?" "What do you use to kill your crab grass?" They never once wonder why they are alive in the world; where they fit into the scheme of things; what would be the "good society"; how to account for suffering and evil in human experience; what their ultimate destiny is. It is these latter questions that religion deals with in Scripture, sermons, hymns, prayers, worship, creed, and everyday life situations.

Mixed marriage. Is there any other kind? Even two members of the same congregation think of God in different terms. One feels warmly loved and protected by the Good Shepherd; the other always seems to be just a bit fearful of the almighty Judge even though he says he believes in forgiveness and the mercy of God. Second, there are sometimes greater differences within a denomination than between two denominations. Mr. A. is by far more liberal than most members of his rather conservative denomination; and Mrs. A. was always far more conservative than most of the members in her liberal group. It turns out that Mr. and Mrs. A. are quite compatible, even though technically it could be called a "mixed marriage."

A pastor and his wife come to mind. He was a strongly "orthodox" Lutheran who believed that correct doctrine was of central importance and had a keen interest in theology. His personal religious experience was largely sacramental and liturgical in nature. Meanwhile, his wife, who was also a Lutheran, came from a movement called "pietism" in which personal conversion experience and informal prayer life were supposed to be spontaneous and not structured. She was also very upset that her husband drank beer. Although both sets of in-laws were so relieved that their son and daughter had not married "outside the faith," you and I know that it was basically a *mixed* marriage. They each represented quite a different "style" of religious life.

It is true, nevertheless, that persons marrying within their own religious group have a lower ratio of divorce than those of a so-called mixed marriage. That is a fact.

Point of view: Differences or similarities? Let us assume that a Roman Catholic man and a Lutheran woman are engaged. They could set down the points of belief and morality that they hold in common or agree on in the left column and the points of disagreement or conflict in the right column. It might begin like this:

Similarities	*Differences*
Belief in Trinity	Marriage of clergy
Infant Baptism	Birth control
Ten Commandments	Antenuptial agreement

Forgiveness	Attitude toward
Prayer	authority of the pope
Old and New	Confirmation seen as a
Testament	sacrament
Divinity of Christ	Anointing of the sick
The Apostles' Creed	The Council of Trent
The Nicene Creed	The Smalcald Articles

_____   _____

_____   _____

The question the Roman Catholic man and the Lutheran woman in our example need to answer is: Do the similarities outweigh the differences? Obviously if the Lutheran woman says, "I love him so much I'll have as many children as he wants (give or take the rhythm method)," then the fact that their denominations have made different official statements about birth control does not really matter. On the other hand, if a great fight is going to develop over which denomination the children should be baptized and confirmed in, that is quite another matter. Add to that the possibility that each set of relatives will be a cheering section, and you have not only a mixed marriage but a tug of war. What would King Solomon have recommended?

Ironically, some couples feel as embarrassed talking about religion and their deep personal beliefs as they do talking about sex, if not more so. Once again, we repeat a basic principle that has run through our discussion of engagement like a red thread:

Discuss all important areas of your life together now freely and frankly; it is better to know now where you stand than to be surprised later by problems for which you are not prepared.

Religious practices can be shared before marriage. Do you go to church and worship together? Is church life and membership in a congregation what you look forward to?

If you do not both belong now to the same church, why not bring your membership into union before the marriage. One of the most rewarding experiences I ever had in premarital counseling as a parish pastor was when the prospective groom was taking instruction to join the church prior to their marriage. We three had many fruitful discussions, and actually the couple came much closer together because of it.

A "church home" is more than a liturgical place of worship. It is also a fellowship (the Apostles' Creed calls it "the communion of saints") of persons who are concerned about one another for Christ's sake. Here are fellow members of the body of Christ who share joys and sorrows, problems and victories.

> Bear one another's burdens, and so fulfill the law of Christ.   (Gal. 6:2)

> For where two or three are gathered in My name, there am I in the midst of them.   (Matt. 18:20)

> So then you are no longer strangers and sojourners, but you are fellow citizens with the saints and members of the household of God, built upon the foundation of the apostles and prophets, Christ Jesus Himself being the chief Cornerstone, in whom the whole structure is joined together and grows into a holy temple in the Lord, in whom you also are built into it for a dwelling place of God in the Spirit.
>
> (Eph. 2:19-22)

If church membership as husband and wife and later as family means anything like that last citation from Ephesians, then there is no question of where one belongs in the world. Such a one is joined into a universal and historic community summed up best in the words of the canticle *Te Deum Laudamus* ("We praise Thee, O God"):

Holy, holy, holy, Lord God of Sabaoth!
Heaven and earth are full of the majesty of Thy glory.
The glorious company of the apostles praise Thee;
The goodly fellowship of the prophets praise Thee;
The noble army of martyrs praise Thee;
The holy church throughout all the world doth
acknowledge Thee:
The Father of an infinite majesty. (Matins)

If this is what you mean by religious perspective and church membership, you have a wonderfully strengthening context in which to live your personal as well as your family life. Such a world view puts everything in proper perspective. Priorities have a way of finding their appropriate significance and value.

A chance to reach out is offered by the church, a protection against becoming too in-grown as a couple and as a family. In our mobile society it is easy to follow the path of least resistance and just sit on your patio in the shade. The church calls us to be concerned for the world about us, for the aged when we ourselves are not aged, for the hungry and sick when we are doing quite well thank you. Our spiritual and compassionate capacities are exercised by the call of high religion to reach out in love to others. This by no means detracts from the love of husband and wife for each other as some fear.

What kind of balance do you two agree on? In a large city church it would be possible to be at a church meeting or worthwhile service project every night to the neglect of marriage and family. You do not need to plan out your schedule for the next 40 years, naturally, but you must have some thoughts on the matter and some preferences. Talk about it.

What of your own prayer and devotional life? Most people let this develop by chance or not develop by neglect.

Again it is up to you. How large a part of your marriage will or can this be?

Finally, concerning religion, be open to growth and development. Just as you progressed beyond third-grade arithmetic and spelling, let your spiritual life mature and grow up. These words from the prayer of blessing at confirmation mean a lot to me still:

> The Father in Heaven, for Jesus's sake, renew and increase in thee the gift of the Holy Ghost, to thy strengthening in faith, to thy *growth in grace,* to thy patience in suffering, and to the blessed hope of everlasting life.
>
> (*Service Book and Hymnal,* p. 246)

PART III

GETTING MARRIED

So many people have a stake in your getting married that you wouldn't believe it. A Catholic priest once told a couple that was all "up tight" about the church wedding plans, "Relax, after all, the wedding is for your folks, the honeymoon is for you two." Even though he was saying this partly in jest to calm their fussing about details, there was a lot of truth in it.

The wedding is the social, ceremonial, and public side of getting married. In that sense it is for the benefit of society. Now everyone knows for sure that your new relationship is quite all right, that you are entitled to live in the same apartment or house, and that you have publicly declared you will be responsible for any children that may come from this union. The Board of Public Welfare heaves a sigh of relief and says, "Good! another solid family on the tax roles. We congratulate you and welcome you into the adult world of Jefferson County." Your folks heave a sigh of relief and say, "Now they are on their own. That wedding set us back a pretty penny, but it was worth every bit of it." All these other people benefit from the public side of your marriage. Even your friends have a good time, staying at the reception long after you are gone, drinking up what is left of the champagne or punch.

The other side of your marriage is the honeymoon when you will "consummate" the marriage in the bridal suite on your wedding night. That is right; until you two are "wedded" in sexual union, the marriage is not complete and even legal. You have read in the newspaper where some underage couple ran off and got married before the justice of the peace. Then they were returned to their homes by some juvenile authority before they had intercourse, or they got scared and ran home. Later it was announced in the paper that their marriage was "annulled" (Webster's synonyms—cancel, nullify, invalidate); no divorce needed because they were never 100 percent married. So, you see, marriage has a private, very personal side, a ceremony at which you two officiate. As the priest mentioned above said, "I don't really marry you; you marry each other."

Now we want to consider both the public and the private aspects of your marriage.

CHAPTER 11

The Wedding

No one blames you for getting all excited and filled with anticipation as your wedding day draws nearer and your engagement will come to an end. The whole reason for your engagement has been to get ready for the big day, and beyond.

Notice how the tempo is building up? Shopping for dresses for bridesmaids, where to rent a tuxedo, oh, yes, and black shoes. What about the guest list, and the cake, and the flowers, and the flower girl (whose niece?), and where to hide the car so Joe won't short the starter motor, and nobody told us we had to reserve the church—say, you don't suppose we set the date in the middle of a menstrual period for heaven's sake?

Some of the fussy stuff can be avoided by a little fore-thought and careful planning. But if you think you can or should get through a wedding without any excitement, you are as foolish as the farmer who wanted to attend the county fair when there was no crowd. A wedding is sup-posed to be a festive occasion, a gala celebration, rejoicing among relatives and friends, as many as can come.

Begin at the beginning. Talk to the clergyman well in advance. He is a professional and likely an old hand at marrying. He can get you started on the right foot—scheduling what is needed, what is necessary, what is helpful.

There will be plenty of opportunity for individual

preferences. And do not decide arbitrarily in advance what you can and cannot have included.

Maybe you are as hard up financially as one couple I married. He was a navy recruit from far away. She, the daughter of a poor family that could not possibly put on much of a reception for the young couple. The women's group in the church gathered flowers from their gardens for bouquets and served coffee and punch with cake and cookies in the church basement after the ceremony. It was one of the most fun gatherings I've attended. Many of the members attended, partly to make up for the fact that the fellow's folks were unable to make the long trip. How unfortunate if this couple would have thought they "could not afford a church wedding" and had stood up in city hall all by themselves!

More elaborate and expensive weddings are perfectly fine if they are within the financial means of the family. The point is there can be wonderfully good feeling in any setting providing everyone means well and is considerate. There are plenty of good etiquette and bridal books to guide a couple through the most complicated and elaborate forms of entertaining. Grace and good manners are appropriate anytime, especially at a gala celebration like a wedding. So live it up!

Just one word of caution. Do not let the arrangements and scheduling get you down. What is the good of elaborate plans to have a good time if you pass out from nervous exhaustion halfway through? What good is a beautiful wedding and reception if you have a sick headache the first three days of your honeymoon? or get in a bad temper and snap at each other? or can no longer speak to the rest of your family? So, lay plans in advance and "take it easy"; avoid unnecessary complications.

One way to save a lot of wasted energy and to help things run smoothly is to have only one umpire in this ball game, for the ceremony at least. Your clergyman has an "Order for Marriage" in his *Occasional Services Book* or church worship book (every denomination has). Let him guide you through it and explain it as he feels necessary. This part is the worship service and not a final examination in a course on etiquette nor a rehearsal for a "coming out" debut. You have managed to get down the aisle for Holy Communion without much rehearsing; chances are all you need is a little coordinating and a little suggestion on where to place yourselves before the altar to make everything most convenient. Any rehearsals I have seen or participated in that took a nerve-wrackingly long time could have been made so much simpler if the people would have let themselves be ministered to.

Give yourself the chance to enter into the spirit of the marriage ceremony. Some of the Scripture passages used take a deeper meaning even though you have heard them many times before. For example:

> The Lord God said: It is not good that the man should be alone; I will make him a help meet for him. . . . Husbands, love your wives, even as Christ loved the church and gave Himself for it.

And later, taking each other's hand:

> I, _____, take thee, _____, to be my wedded wife/husband, to have and to hold from this day forward, for better or worse, for richer or poorer, in sickness and in health, to love and to cherish, till death us do part.

What a promise!

Oh, by the way, the state has some requirements too, you know. There is the matter of the marriage license, which is a legal document indicating that you fulfill the qualifications of age, health, etc. As we said, society has a stake in your marriage. In advance of getting your license you should have seen a physician for a premarital examination (both of you, and even if your state does not require it), a blood test, and anything else required by local law.

Let the premarital physical examination be an opportunity for you to ask your physician any final questions you have about sex, childbirth, health, anything else you feel is in his province to counsel you about. Take the initiative in talking to him since he may feel you would be satisfied with, and even desire, only the minimum legally required examination and blood test. Occasionally some impediment to marital adjustment can be easily cleared up if this examination takes place well in advance of the wedding.

So now you are ready to get married. Have a good time at your wedding. Congratulations! Best wishes! Bon voyage!

CHAPTER 12

The Honeymoon

It's a good idea to plan your honeymoon before your wedding—during your engagement. Or if you want to, the groom-to-be can plan it as a surprise for the bride-to-be. So much is unpredictable on a honeymoon that it's a relief to have some things fixed and certain. Like where to stay each night. It's good to know there's a room reserved at the end of each day's travel or sight-seeing or visiting.

What is a honeymoon for? It is an opportunity to give yourself the best possible start on your actual married life together. Therefore, it should have certain built-in arrangements: privacy, fun, relaxation after the busy preparations for the wedding, sex of course, something special, interesting new activities but not too busy and crowded a schedule, not so expensive you will regret it later (like for the next 24 months at the loan company), but the kind of vacation that is worth splurging on a bit, not so short that you won't feel you have "been away," yet not so long that time drags and you are impatient about getting your household settled.

At the risk of sticking my neck out and trying hard to restrain myself from telling you exactly what kind of honeymoon you should have (as though I knew), let us look further at what all is involved.

The man camping enthusiast may take his bride-to-be at face value when she agrees to tenting on their honeymoon, but neither has taken into account that she may not feel her most feminine bridelike self in a sleeping bag. How about a combination beginning in a hotel or motel near the state park with outings of camping interspersed?

Travel is another factor worth thinking about. Pushing 400 or 500 miles between motel reservations can be hard work. Save that kind of trip for later when you are a bit more used to each other and maybe have more time. The first night, especially if you are having an evening or late afternoon wedding, see if you can find a nice place to stay within an hour or two of driving time. You need some time to relax and unwind before retiring for the evening.

The wedding night! What high hopes of unspeakable bliss. I hope you won't think me a spoilsport if I ask you to lower your expectations and sexual fantasies just a little bit. You see, it is precisely overexpectation that leads to frustration and disappointment. Rather take the attitude that you are entering a relationship which will grow and develop as you live together. Chances are the third night or a week later you will have a better sexual union than on the wedding night following all the excitement and long day of festivities. That is precisely why the honeymoon should maybe be a week or so. But that is not all. If your marriage follows anywhere near the development of most of us, sexual relations become richer, more passionate, and more satisfying as years go by. Therefore, it is unfortunate to stake all one's hopes on the wedding night.

Do not let anything I have said so far dissuade you from being spontaneous and enthusiastic on your trip. The purpose behind planning in advance and other considerations is that your joy may be maximum and the beginning days of your marriage be as positive and happy as possible. It is a wonderful time of life!

Here are a few things you might like to check off in regard to your honeymoon plans:

_____ Time off from work and sufficient arrangements so

that you can leave business and other worries behind you.

____ Reservations in advance and double-checked.

____ Budgeting so you do not show up financially embarrassed (the man's concern).

____ Enough discussion so both will be happy with the arrangements even though the woman might say, "It's up to you, Jack." *GOOD THOUGHT*

____ Suitable clothing for whatever you plan to do (from canoeing to going out to dinner).

____ Planned parenthood starts now if that is your agreement (better not each assume the other has provided for it).

____ Did you fill the gas tank?

____ Like we said before, "Have fun!"

DISCUSS-O-GRAPH

Fill yours out before you look at mine to compare

Turn to the back of this book. You will find two pages on which you can record your attitudes and opinions about a number of items under the five headings of Part II, "Have You Talked About It?"

You will notice that there is one form for the man and one for the woman. Tear out both sheets, but fill out the graphs separately. Then you may compare them.

The point is not to find some "correct" answer that I might have in mind. Answer exactly as you genuinely feel or believe it applies to you. Do not even guess what your partner might write in order to make sure you agree. I do not care whether you agree or not, but I am concerned that you know how each of you reacts to an assortment of significant questions. What you do with the agreement or disagreement is entirely up to you. At least you will want to discuss the results.

Social Relations

1. Our parents trust us and treat us like adults.
2. Our families have about the same social-economic standing in the community.
3. It is essential to the "good life" to have a college education.
4. We agree on the kinds of organizations (social, political,

economic) to which we would like to belong in the future.

5. I wish we would attend more parties and double-date more frequently.

6. If most people on welfare worked hard and set their mind to it, they could make a success of their lives.

7. My friends think we should get married.

8. The man in this couple has very acceptable manners and gets along comfortably in social situations.

9. The woman in this couple is a competent and gracious hostess.

10. We enjoy the same hobbies and recreational activities.

Economic-Vocational

1. I definitely want a joint checking account.

2. We should be on the bond-a-month plan or in some other way save so much each month from the beginning of marriage.

3. It is morbid to make out a will when we are both so young and healthy.

4. Both husband and wife should carry life insurance.

5. The man in this couple has a fine job and has maybe gone about as far as he can vocationally.

6. We disagree over what is "stingy" and what is "wasteful."

7. A budget is not necessary since we both have good common sense about money.

8. Our ideas about working mothers are in agreement.

9. It would be good if the man in this couple were more ambitious to improve his job situation by more education or training.

10. It is quite all right to borrow up to $500 for a nice vacation since "all work and no play makes Jack a dull boy."

Personality

1. The man in this couple sometimes holds back and does not express his real feelings for fear of criticism by his partner.
2. The woman in this couple sometimes holds back and does not express her real feelings for fear of criticism by her partner.
3. We are both about equally mature in our personalities.
4. The man should be the more aggressive and dominant person as the head of the family.
5. We have clashes of mood and temperament that are damaging to our relationship.
6. We are flexible enough to compromise and resolve our differences most of the time.
7. I wish we had more of a mutual sense of humor.
8. I wish we had more sensitivity and spontaneity in our relationship. We are more or less in a rut already.
9. We need help in improving our communication with each other.
10. I prefer more of a set schedule, specific plans, and promptness than my partner.

Sexuality

1. Having children "cramps the style" of a married couple.
2. Sex is more appreciated by a man than a woman generally.
3. We have already gone farther in sexual intimacy than I believe we should have.
4. I want the same number of children as my partner.
5. I had a wholesome explanation about human sexuality from my parents and plan to give the same to my children.
6. I am lacking in sex education and am a bit uneasy about the sex side of marriage.

7. The church is too strict in requiring fidelity forever in marriage.
8. Sexual incompatibility is sufficient grounds for divorce.
9. Sexual relations cease at menopause (climacteric) in middle age.
10. Since I am sure I could never be tempted to be unfaithful to my spouse, I do not need to take special precautions in my relationship with the opposite sex.

Religious Perspective

1. The church is not relevant to the major problems of our modern world.
2. The will of God is of great importance to me as I make decisions in my life.
3. We should wait with joining a local church till we know how long we are going to be living in the community.
4. We both have about the same degree of faith and/or doubt in our religious orientation.
5. I am sure both sets of parents will attend the wedding.
6. I believe we should look to the Bible for guidance in matters of faith and life because it is the authority.
7. We should have grace at meals, Scripture reading, and prayer together in our home.
8. We plan to join the same church or religious group.
9. We agree on the same basic moral standards (traffic laws, honesty, fulfilling obligations and commitments, gossip, use of alcohol, sexual behavior, etc.).
10. We are agreed on and pleased about the plans for our church wedding.

ENGAGEMENT DISCUSS-O-GRAPH

Woman's Form

Social Relations	Economic-Vocational	Personality	Sexuality	Religious Perspective
1.	1.	1.	1.	1.
2.	2.	2.	2.	2.
3.	3.	3.	3.	3.
4.	4.	4.	4.	4.
5.	5.	5.	5.	5.
6.	6.	6.	6.	6.
7.	7.	7.	7.	7.
8.	8.	8.	8.	8.
9.	9.	9.	9.	9.
10.	10.	10.	10.	10.

If you agree with an item, circle the number. If you disagree, leave it blank.

ENGAGEMENT DISCUSS-O-GRAPH

Man's Form

Social Relations	Economic-Vocational	Personality	Sexuality	Religious Perspective
(1.)	(1.)	(1.)	(1.)	1.
2.	(2.)	2.	2.	(2.)
3.	3.	(3.)	3.	(3.)
4.	(4.)	4.	4.	4.
(5.)	5.	5.	(5.)	(5.)
(6.)	6.	(6.)	(6.)	(6.)
(7.)	7.	7.	7.	(7.)
(8.)	(8.)	8.	8.	(8.)
(9.)	9.	(9.)	9.	9.
(10.)	10.	(10.)	10.	(10.)

If you agree with an item, circle the number. If you disagree, leave it blank.